Mind, Body, Relax:
Puzzles and Mindfulness for Adults

This Book Belongs To:

____

TKTCollection

ON THE GO

Book

TKTCollection

ON THE GO

Books

Copyright ©December 2023 TKTCollection Publishing.

Mind, Body, Relax:

Puzzles and Mindfulness for Adults

Independently Published By:

TKTCollection

ISBN: 978-1-959247-26-5

Date: 2023

Copyright © December 2023 TKTCollection Publishing. All Rights Reserved. No part of the publication may be used or reproduced, distributed, or transmitted, in any form or by any means, including photocopying, recording, or other electronic or mechanical methods, without the publisher's written permission tktcollection.com

Welcome to TKTCollection's 'On the Go' Book-
Mind Body Relax: Puzzles and Mindfulness for Adults.

Fun meets relaxation and mental stimulation, so get your coloring pencils or pens ready because this book offers a delightful blend of intricate puzzles, brain teasers, and soothing coloring pages.

Whether you're a Sudoku enthusiast, a crossword wizard, or enjoy mindful coloring, there's something here for you.

Perfect for those quiet moments during travels or when you want to unwind and take a break from the hustle and bustle of daily life. Explore diverse topics like travel, literature, and health while engaging in activities that will challenge your mind and promote relaxation. So, sit back, relax, and immerse yourself in a world of puzzles, games, and creative expression!

Color Test Page

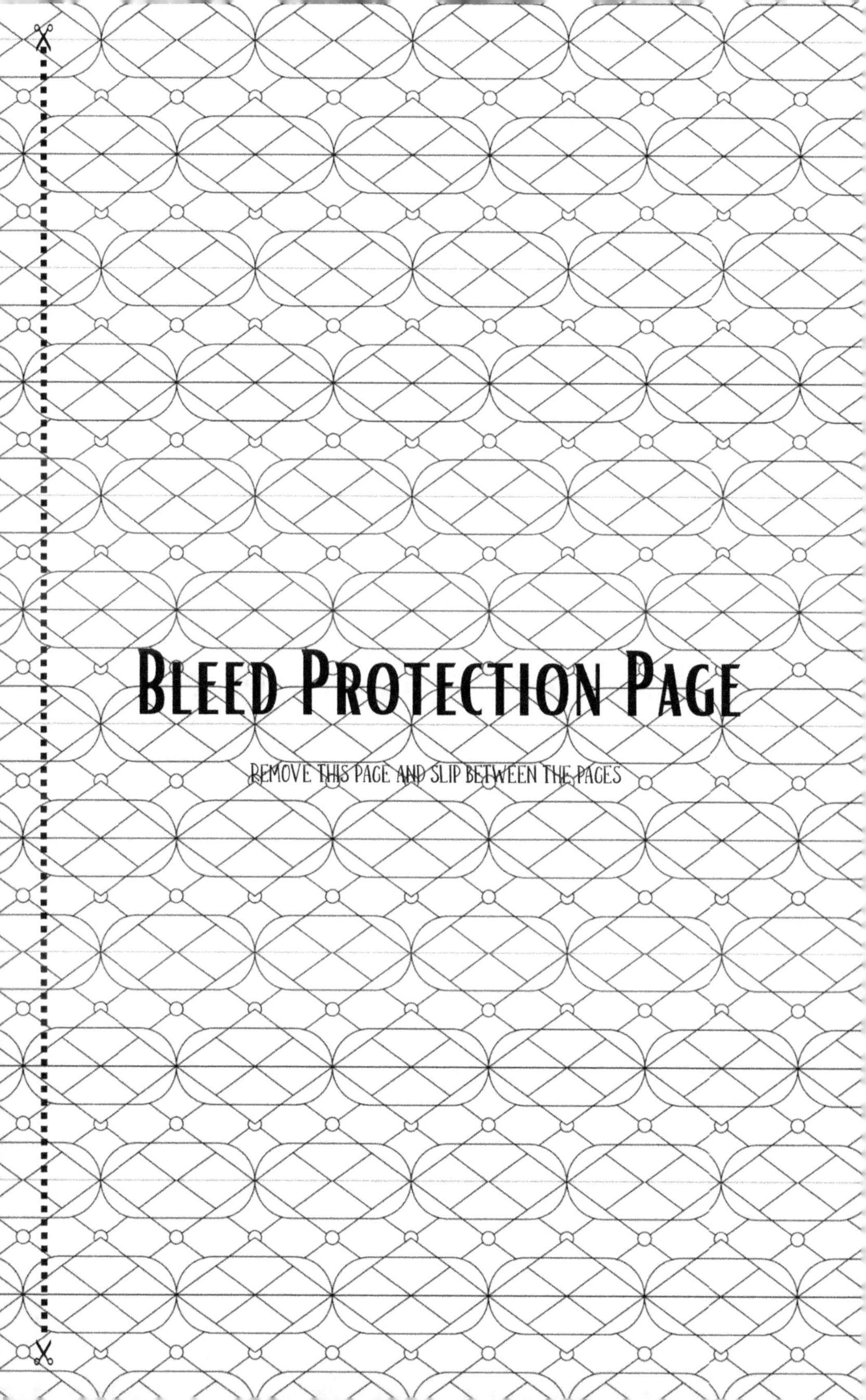
BLEED PROTECTION PAGE
REMOVE THIS PAGE AND SLIP BETWEEN THE PAGES

Bleed Protection Page

Remove this page and slip between the pages

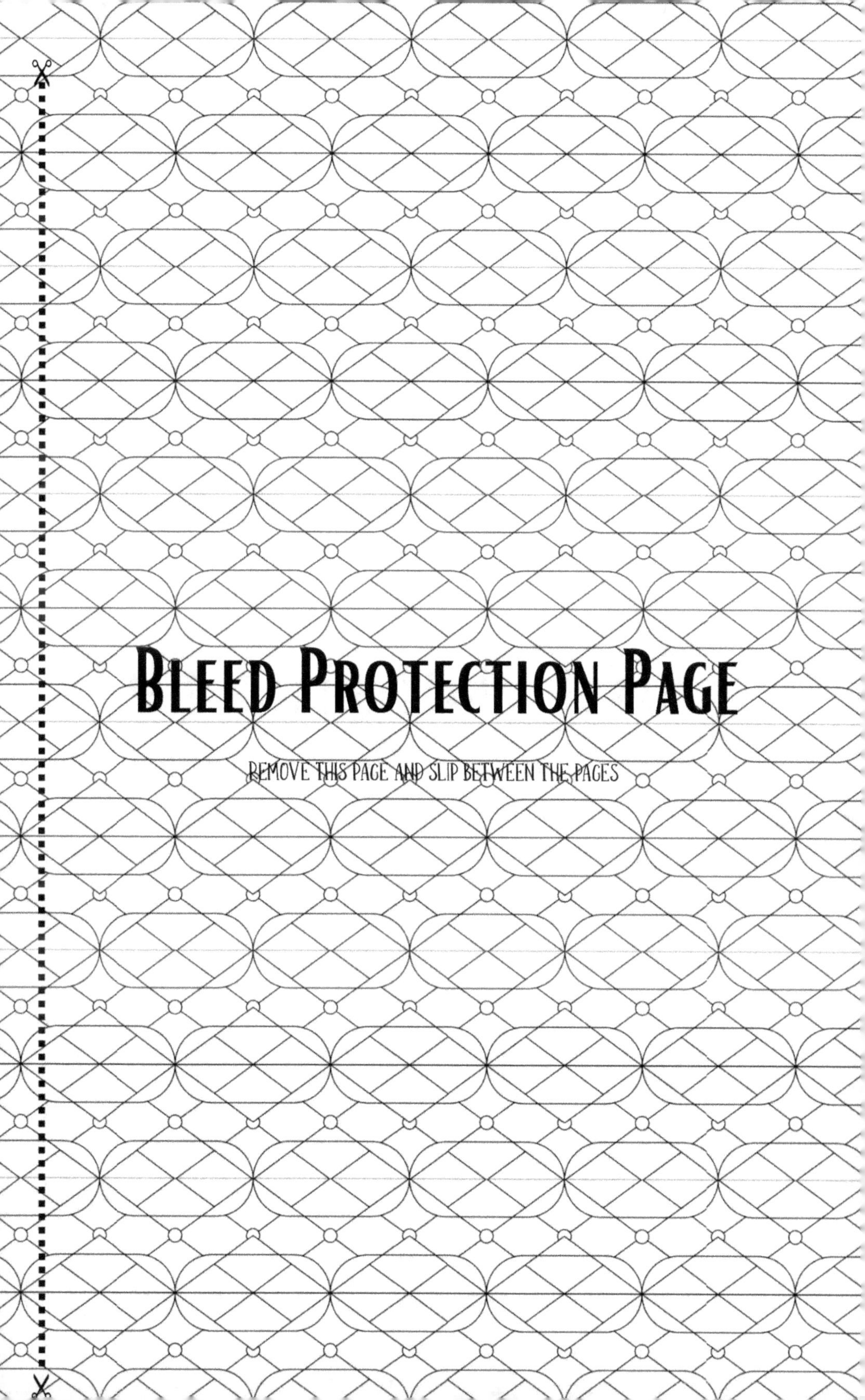

Bleed Protection Page
Remove this page and slip between the pages

Bleed Protection Page
Remove this page and slip between the pages

Positivity

O	M	M	P	D	Y	G	N	P	J	J	Y	N	F	G	F	G
H	A	P	P	R	E	C	I	A	T	I	O	N	A	L	X	N
H	P	B	J	T	R	E	C	G	R	D	W	A	A	E	E	I
S	I	Z	N	Y	K	A	P	R	E	N	F	N	S	K	W	H
E	E	T	I	W	L	M	J	G	Y	F	O	U	F	E	F	T
C	Y	W	N	M	M	G	U	C	I	I	C	N	X	V	I	A
N	T	Z	I	V	M	U	H	R	T	O	R	E	D	N	M	E
A	E	N	E	F	E	I	M	O	F	G	R	L	N	T	T	R
L	G	H	L	J	N	A	M	K	R	C	C	E	E	U	E	B
A	N	W	X	T	T	E	I	O	I	L	R	C	I	V	D	C
B	O	E	D	I	A	P	U	S	A	P	H	Q	I	Z	D	A
S	P	Z	O	D	L	N	E	R	E	N	G	T	B	W	L	U
N	C	N	C	I	D	S	I	A	I	Q	I	X	X	U	J	A
L	S	X	Y	I	F	T	C	Q	H	S	P	G	R	C	B	J
V	N	E	N	Z	Y	E	U	G	O	G	O	A	G	X	N	V
S	C	G	F	B	A	E	O	P	Y	V	G	E	G	J	F	F
Z	R	V	G	F	S	N	A	U	H	C	X	T	S	O	U	D

affirmations	appreciation	balance
breathing	calming	clarity
deep	emotional	exercises
focus	grounding	inner peace
mental	positive	techniques

Vision Board

Vision Board

Body Scan

Find a comfortable and quiet place to sit or lie down.
Close your eyes and take a few deep breaths to relax.

- Start by bringing your attention to your toes. Notice any sensations, tension, or relaxation in your toes. Take a deep breath in and as you exhale, release any tension in this area.
- Gradually move your focus up through your feet, ankles, calves, knees, thighs, and so on, bringing awareness to each body part.
- With each breath, imagine sending relaxation and calmness to that specific body part.
- Continue scanning through your body, acknowledging any sensations without judgment.
- Finally, bring your attention to your entire body as a whole. Notice how you feel and embrace a sense of relaxation and peace.

I Am Thankful For

Write 3 things you are thankful for today.

#1

#2

#3

Bee Amazing

On The Go
Books
TRT Collection Publishing

Completed By:

Date:

Sudoku

LEVEL: Easy

	7				1		4	5
			4			6	1	
	4	1						
		9	5	8	6		3	
3	8			1	4	7	5	
		2	9	7	3			6
1		7	3	4				
5			8	6	9			
		3				9		4

Notes

Finger Labyrinth

You can use your finger to trace the path to the labyrinth's center slowly.

Focus your breathing, calm and slowly, as you trace to the center. When you reach the center, draw in 3 long, deep breaths.

Then, trace the path back to the outside. Repeat until you feel focused and calm.

Which Doesn't Belong

Harmony

I	E	Z	B	R	C	M	A	R	E	N	N	I	P	M	U	X
B	T	B	T	R	O	G	Y	O	F	O	A	U	J	Y	O	U
G	L	R	B	E	O	E	N	J	Z	E	M	F	T	N	S	B
R	W	H	S	Y	L	P	O	J	O	E	R	T	F	F	S	M
A	S	F	L	C	N	W	M	A	N	X	Y	S	V	V	E	N
T	R	Z	T	P	Y	M	R	T	X	P	B	U	U	J	N	X
I	R	E	X	R	H	T	A	A	H	P	X	B	P	Z	I	T
T	E	A	L	R	I	L	H	K	M	E	I	M	B	R	P	D
U	S	M	A	I	B	L	E	I	G	P	D	V	P	C	P	J
D	I	Q	O	O	E	U	E	N	O	U	H	I	T	G	A	Y
E	L	H	R	T	A	F	R	D	V	E	C	A	E	P	H	T
A	I	B	M	R	I	Y	L	Q	R	K	L	L	Y	D	T	F
C	E	K	B	P	I	O	O	A	Q	E	L	I	H	C	W	M
K	N	N	F	P	B	J	N	X	Z	J	A	I	M	U	H	D
E	C	W	P	G	M	X	M	A	Y	C	E	M	B	C	A	K
E	E	N	S	K	T	P	A	W	L	P	K	R	D	T	M	X
O	M	O	Z	T	U	B	W	S	S	E	N	L	L	E	W	Y

dream
happiness
joyful
relief
yoga

emotional
harmony
mental
resilience

gratitude
inner
peace
wellness

Empowerment Journey

I am strong, capable, and worthy of success.

"Your present circumstances don't determine where you can go; they merely determine where you start."
- Nido Qubein

Empowerment Affirmations

Affirmations are powerful statements that can shape your mindset and beliefs. Take a moment to create your own empowering affirmations or mantras.

- Write down empowering statements or phrases that resonate with you.
- Ensure they are present-tense, positive, and personal

These affirmations serve as positive reminders to boost confidence, resilience, and self-belief in your daily life.

#1

#2

#3

Examples

"I embrace challenges as opportunities for growth"

"I radiate confidence and attract positivity into my life."

"I trust in my ability to overcome obstacles with grace."

Sudoku

LEVEL: Easy

3	6			1				
7			4				6	
8		1			5		7	3
		7	3	5		2		
	9			8	1		5	
5			7	6	9	8		
		8		9	2			1
2			8	7	6			
	7	5			3			

Notes

I Am Thankful For

Write 3 things you are thankful for today.

#1

#2

#3

On The Go
Books

TRT Collection Publishing

Completed By:

Date:

Trail of Confidence

"Believe in yourself and all that you are. Know that there is something inside you that is greater than any obstacle." - Christian D. Larson

Self Portrait

Upper Body Scan

Upper Body Scans focus on the neck, shoulders, arms, and hands.

Whether you're commuting on a train or bus, at work, or taking a quick break, the Upper Body Scan exercise is your go-to for instant relaxation.

Focus on your neck, shoulders, arms, and hands to release stress and promote a sense of calmness during your busy day.

Take a moment to unwind and relieve tension in these areas with simple, mindful exercises that can easily fit into your daily routine.

I Am Thankful For

Write 3 things you are thankful for today.

#1

#2

#3

Sudoku

LEVEL: Hard

9	1				6	2		
	7		1		3	5		
4		2						
	3			5	7			1
6			3					
5			7			1	9	
			4					8
		7		8				

Notes

Strength Maze Quest

"You are never too old to set another goal or to dream a new dream." - C.S. Lewis

On The Go
Books
TR T Collection Publishing

Completed By:

Date:

Movie Cryptogram

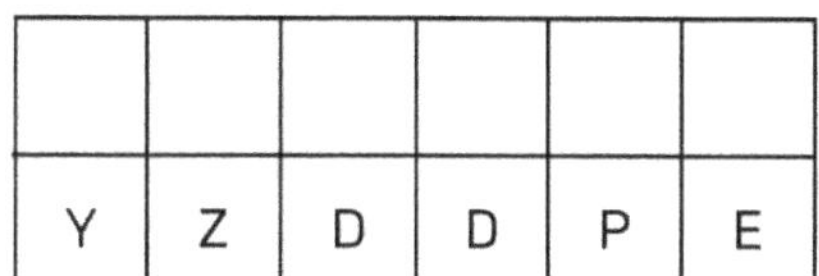

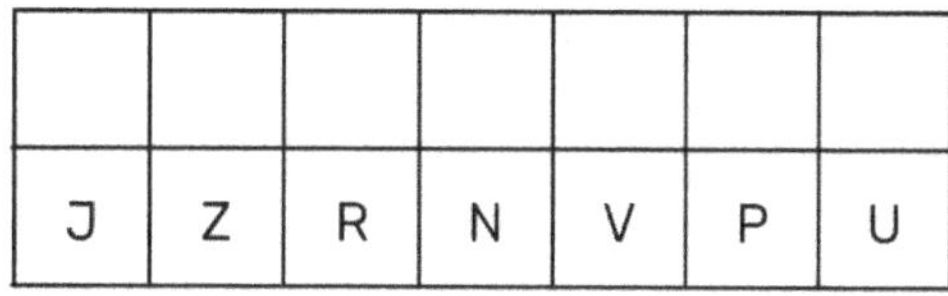

Clue:

Trailblazing Mathematicians in NASA

Notes

Self Criticism Worksheet

Critical Thought/s

What Triggered the Thought/s?

Any Physical and/or Emotional Sensations?

Letting Go Of

I am capable

Self Criticism

Self Criticism Worksheet

Compassionate Thought

What would you say to a friend who expressed this thought?

A Year From Now

How will you feel about this event new year?

Concrete Plan

What actions can you take to prepare for this in the future?

Big Picture Plan

Imagine a future, free of this thought. What would you do?

Sudoku

LEVEL: Medium

5	1	4			7		3	
	9			5		4	1	
	8	2				6	7	
		5	9		6			4
1	3							
9	4		5	8				
					4	8		1
				6	3			
4	2			1				3

Notes

On The Go Books

TR TCollection Publishing

Completed By:

Date:

Courageous Pathways

"The only limit to our realization of tomorrow will be our doubts of today." - Franklin D. Roosevelt

Lower Body Scan

Direct your focus to your hips, thighs, lower legs, and feet.

Soothe muscles and cultivate a sense of relaxation. With simple, mindful exercises tailored for your lower body, find a moment of tranquility and ease wherever you are in your daily routine.

Letter to Your Future Self

Serenity

Z	A	B	S	C	A	N	U	F	Z	K	J	S	D	E	A	M
N	X	B	I	E	X	E	R	C	I	S	E	S	Z	F	Y	A
M	A	P	P	R	E	C	I	A	T	I	O	N	S	V	A	B
R	M	E	B	N	L	L	G	I	Z	U	W	S	T	D	I	S
W	A	T	G	Z	T	A	O	R	M	F	E	V	R	F	Y	N
B	E	W	Z	K	G	R	C	L	O	N	B	R	A	H	B	O
R	R	T	H	F	M	I	F	O	L	U	E	N	N	A	M	I
E	D	P	S	L	Z	T	T	U	X	S	N	P	Q	R	Y	T
A	N	R	T	E	R	Y	F	L	I	C	N	D	U	M	Z	A
T	F	E	F	W	K	D	S	L	I	A	I	Y	I	O	V	M
H	T	L	B	K	N	E	I	M	L	L	G	Y	L	N	T	R
I	F	I	I	I	R	E	M	U	Y	M	S	Y	I	Y	G	I
N	O	E	M	E	N	T	F	V	P	N	Q	D	T	B	O	F
G	G	F	N	C	T	Y	R	I	K	E	D	W	Y	X	S	F
W	T	I	E	I	O	J	D	U	D	S	V	D	P	Q	W	A
S	T	Q	A	J	C	N	F	V	J	S	U	A	E	F	H	W
Y	Q	D	S	D	U	C	S	S	E	N	I	P	P	A	H	M

affirmations
calmness
exercises
harmony
relief
tranquility
appreciation
clarity
grounding
joyful
resilience
breathing
dream
happiness
mindfulness
serenity

Which Doesn't Belong

I Am Thankful For

Write 3 things you are thankful for today.

Anxiety Worksheet

Source of Anxiety: ______________________

____

Physical Sensations: ______________________

____

____

Negative Beliefs

What Helps Me?

What other ways can you see the situation?

What has helped me in the past?

Color the places you feel anxiety.

On The Go Books

TRT Collection Publishing

Completed By:

Date:

Crossword

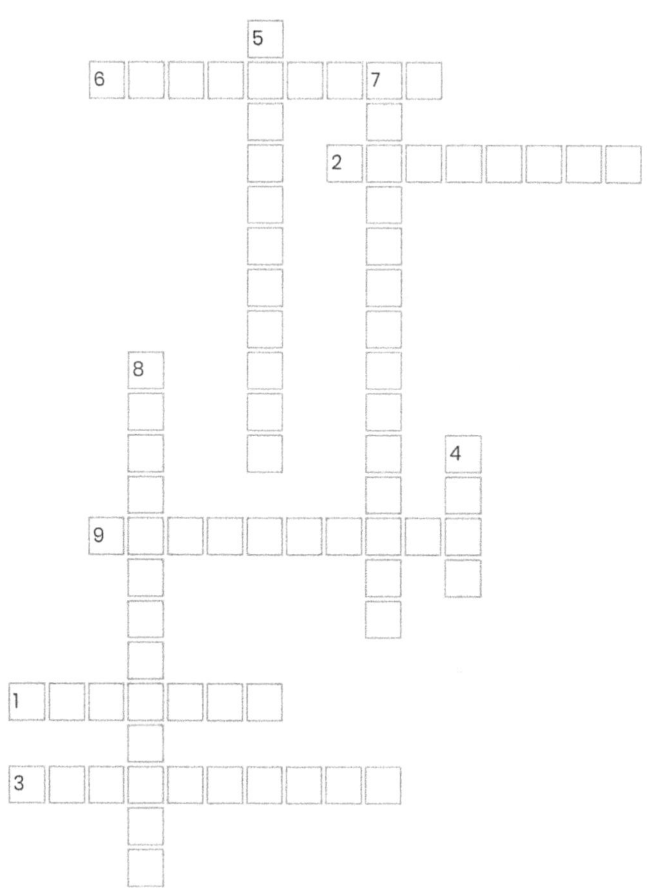

Across

[1] Opposite of stressed.

[2] A state of tranquility.

[3] Breathing and relaxation exercises.

[6] Feeling of appreciation.

[9] State of contentment and satisfaction .

Down

[4] Technique for reducing tension in muscles.

[5] Practise of being present.

[7] Technique involving controlled breathing patterns.

[8] process of mental reflection and introspection.

Sudoku

LEVEL: Medium

7	8		6	2				
	5	3	9			2		
			7				9	6
2	1			5	9	3		8
	4		8		7		2	
3					4		5	
	9				8	6		1
	6			9	2	8		4

Notes

Movie Cryptogram

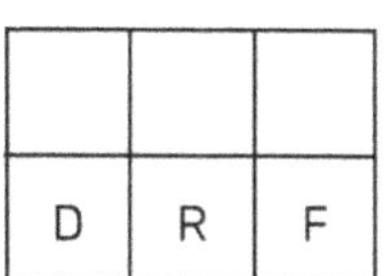

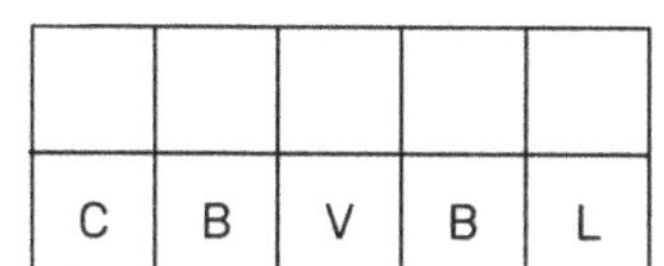

G T L G V F

Clue:

Adaptation of Alice Walker's novel.

Wellness

I	M	M	D	Y	B	R	N	Y	K	Z	W	R	E	R	H	B
F	L	V	O	N	G	Z	G	R	A	T	I	T	U	D	E	R
T	F	G	S	U	Q	H	C	U	R	H	L	D	F	C	V	E
R	A	G	P	E	X	S	S	E	N	M	L	A	C	K	E	A
A	E	R	N	Z	S	J	Q	G	R	B	I	G	S	M	P	T
N	M	E	A	I	W	I	N	G	G	T	I	K	O	Z	W	H
Q	I	S	N	N	D	E	C	W	K	T	J	T	O	V	F	I
U	N	I	G	Z	Y	N	L	R	E	F	I	H	U	U	P	N
I	D	L	H	X	T	P	U	L	E	O	A	S	Z	U	P	G
L	F	I	W	R	I	N	Y	O	N	X	R	D	U	X	N	Y
I	U	E	W	M	N	O	E	A	R	E	E	C	D	S	M	N
T	L	N	U	K	E	X	L	D	X	G	S	B	X	L	R	Z
Y	N	C	O	V	R	F	A	G	W	A	Y	S	A	J	X	L
R	E	E	F	T	E	S	I	Z	E	M	N	T	F	C	P	G
B	S	O	U	H	S	F	C	K	X	H	N	K	P	D	J	A
H	S	E	C	N	E	I	L	I	S	E	R	Z	A	Z	Q	O
I	M	N	S	N	N	J	D	D	M	W	I	Z	O	H	E	Q

breathing
calmness
emotional
exercises
gratitude
grounding
mental resilience
mindfulness
resilience
serenity
tranquility
wellness
yoga

Reflect on a Mindful Moment

Write about a time when you felt fully present and mindful in the moment. Describe the setting, the sensations you experienced, and how being present affected your thoughts and emotions. Consider the impact it had on your well-being, and how you might incorporate more of these mindful moments into your daily life. Reflect on what you learned from that experience and how it influenced your perspective on mindfulness and living in the present

Finger Labyrinth

You can use your finger to trace the path to the labyrinth's center slowly.

Focus your breathing, calm and slowly, as you trace to the center. When you reach the center, draw in 3 long, deep breaths.

Then, trace the path back to the outside. Repeat until you feel focused and calm.

Empowered Passage

"With the new day comes new strength and new thoughts." - Eleanor Roosevelt

I Am Thankful For

Write 3 things you are thankful for today.

#1

#2

#3

Which Doesn't Belong

On The Go
Books
TRT Collection Publishing

Completed By:

Date:

Maze of Fortitude

"Strength does not come from physical capacity. It comes from an indomitable will."
- Mahatma Gandhi

Sudoku

LEVEL: Easy

		3		1			4	5
7		4				2	9	6
5			6	9	4	1		
9	4	5					2	8
		6	8	4		5		
				2	5	6		4
2			4	8		9	6	
	6					3	5	
	3							7

Notes

Movie Cryptogram

O	J	P	C	A	U

O	J	L	Y	P

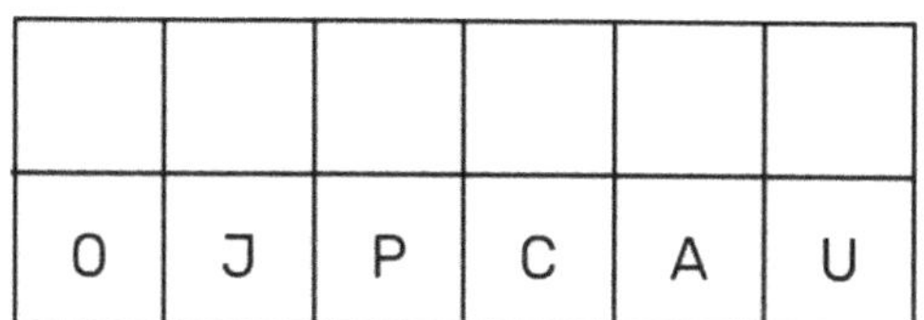

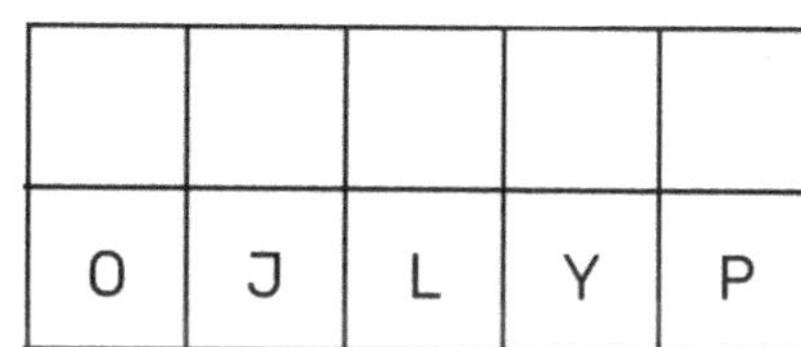

Clue:

Superheroine from Themyscira

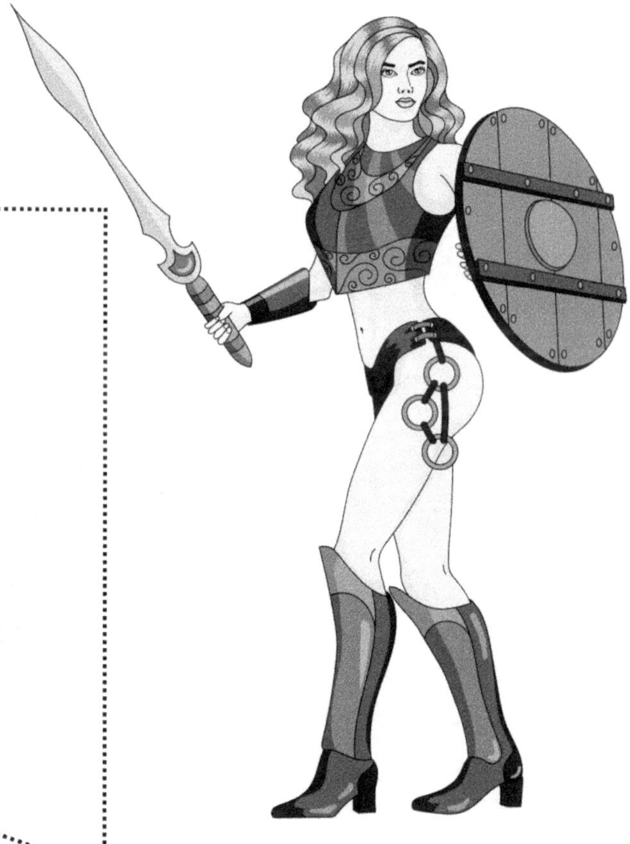

Notes

Self Criticism Worksheet

Critical Thought/s

What Triggered the Thought/s?

Any Physical and/or Emotional Sensations?

Letting Go Of

Self Criticism

Self Criticism Worksheet

Compassionate Thought

What would you say to a friend who expressed this thought?

A Year From Now

How will you feel about this event new year?

Concrete Plan

What actions can you take to prepare for this in the future?

Big Picture Plan

Imagine a future, free of this thought. What would you do?

Crossword

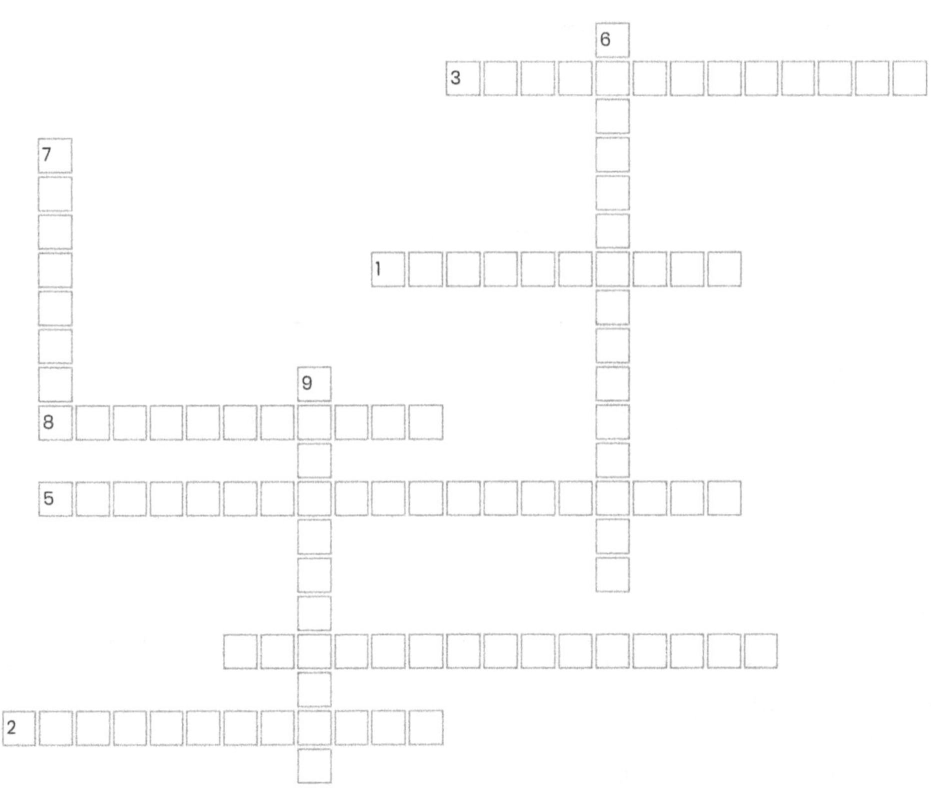

Across

[1] The ability to adapt well to stress and adversity.

[2] A mental state of being grateful or thankful.

[3] The practice of focusing one's mind and eliminating distractions.

[5] A relaxation technique involving controlled breathing.

[8] The state of being mentally and emotionally balanced.

Down

[6] The ability to manage one's emotions and reactions.

[7] A form of physical activity that boosts mental well-being.

[9] A state of inner peace and mental clarity.

Movie Cryptogram

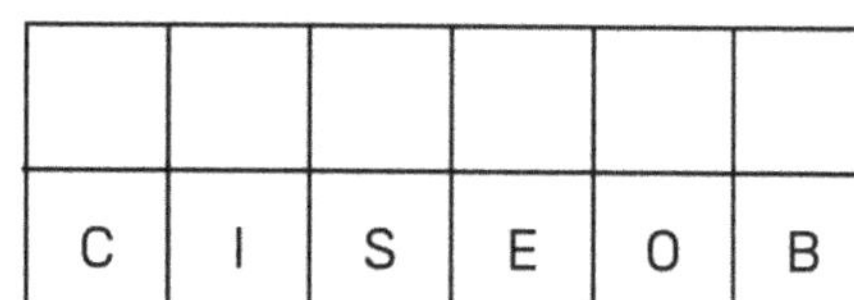

Clue:

Harvard law student's journey.

Balance

O	M	M	P	D	Y	G	N	P	J	J	Y	N	F	G	F	G
H	A	P	P	R	E	C	I	A	T	I	O	N	A	L	X	N
H	P	B	J	T	R	E	C	G	R	D	W	A	A	E	E	I
S	I	Z	N	Y	K	A	P	R	E	N	F	N	S	K	W	H
E	E	T	I	W	L	M	J	G	Y	F	O	U	F	E	F	T
C	Y	W	N	M	M	G	U	C	I	I	C	N	X	V	I	A
N	T	Z	I	V	M	U	H	R	T	O	R	E	D	N	M	E
A	E	N	E	F	E	I	M	O	F	G	R	L	N	T	T	R
L	G	H	L	J	N	A	M	K	R	C	C	E	E	U	E	B
A	N	W	X	T	T	E	I	O	I	L	R	C	I	V	D	C
B	O	E	D	I	A	P	U	S	A	P	H	Q	I	Z	D	A
S	P	Z	O	D	L	N	E	R	E	N	G	T	B	W	L	U
N	C	N	C	I	D	S	I	A	I	Q	I	X	X	U	J	A
L	S	X	Y	I	F	T	C	Q	H	S	P	G	R	C	B	J
V	N	E	N	Z	Y	E	U	G	O	G	O	A	G	X	N	V
S	C	G	F	B	A	E	O	P	Y	V	G	E	G	J	F	F
Z	R	V	G	F	S	N	A	U	H	C	X	T	S	O	U	D

affirmations	appreciation	balance
breathing	calming	clarity
deep	emotional	exercises
focus	grounding	inner peace
mental	positive	techniques

Inner Strength Route

"Success is not final, failure is not fatal: It is the courage to continue that counts." - Winston Churchill

Sudoku

LEVEL: Medium

7	8				4	6		
4		3						
5	6							7
	1				7		2	5
6		7	8		1		9	3
8	5	4						
				8	6	2	7	9
					5		6	
				3	9	5		

Notes

On The Go
Books
TR T Collection Publishing

Completed By:

Date:

Crossword

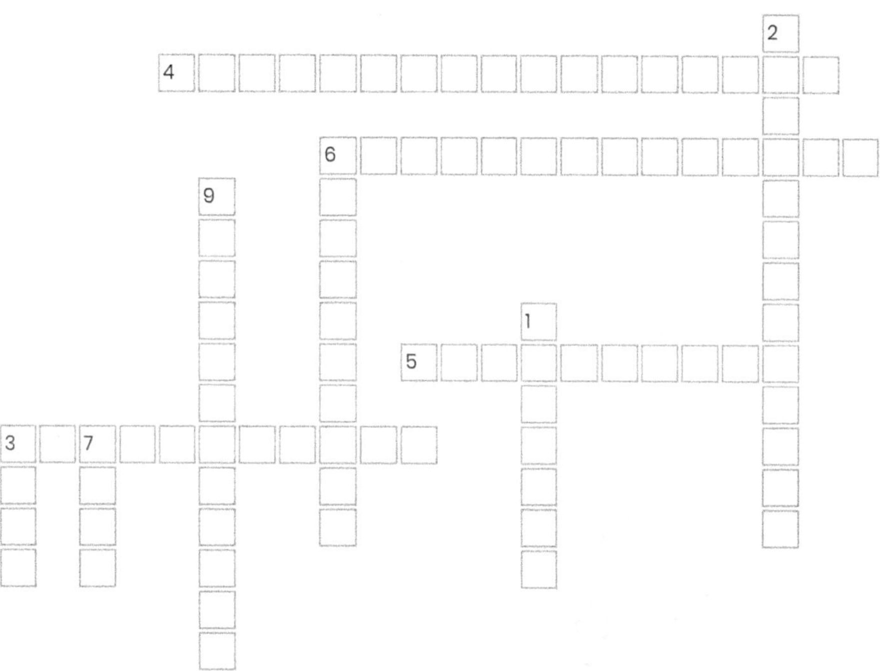

Across

[3] A technique for releasing tension through stretching.

[4] A method of clearing the mind through repetitive actions.

[5] A practice that involves controlled and intentional breathing.

[6] The act of slowing down and being present in the moment.

Down

[1] A technique to alleviate stress through rhythmic movements.

[2] The ability to cope with life's challenges.

[3] A state of being fully immersed and absorbed in an activity.

[6] An approach to reduce stress by simplifying life.

[7] A state of mental and physical relaxation.

[9] The ability to bounce back from difficult experiences.

Movie Cryptogram

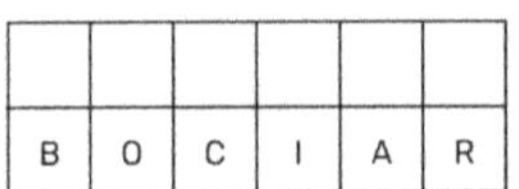

&

I H V Z T C

Clue:

Outlaws on a road trip.

Notes

Finger Labyrinth

You can use your finger to trace the path to the labyrinth's center slowly.

Focus your breathing, calm and slowly, as you trace to the center. When you reach the center, draw in 3 long, deep breaths.

Then, trace the path back to the outside. Repeat until you feel focused and calm.

Anxiety Worksheet

Source of Anxiety: ______________________

____

Physical Sensations: ______________________

____

____

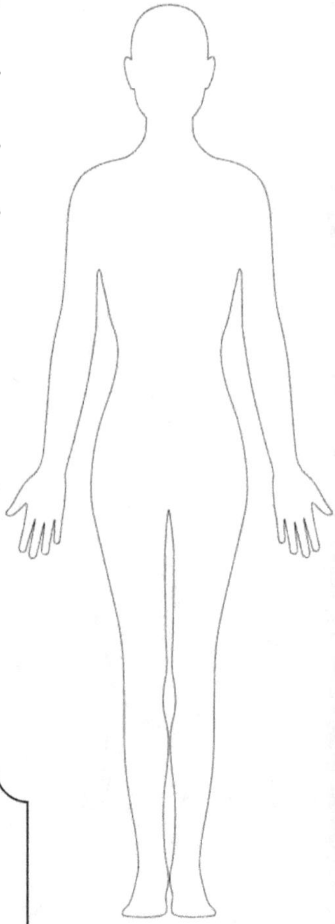

Negative Beliefs

What Helps Me?

What other ways can you see the situation?

What has helped me in the past?

Color the places you feel anxiety.

Trailblazing Confidence

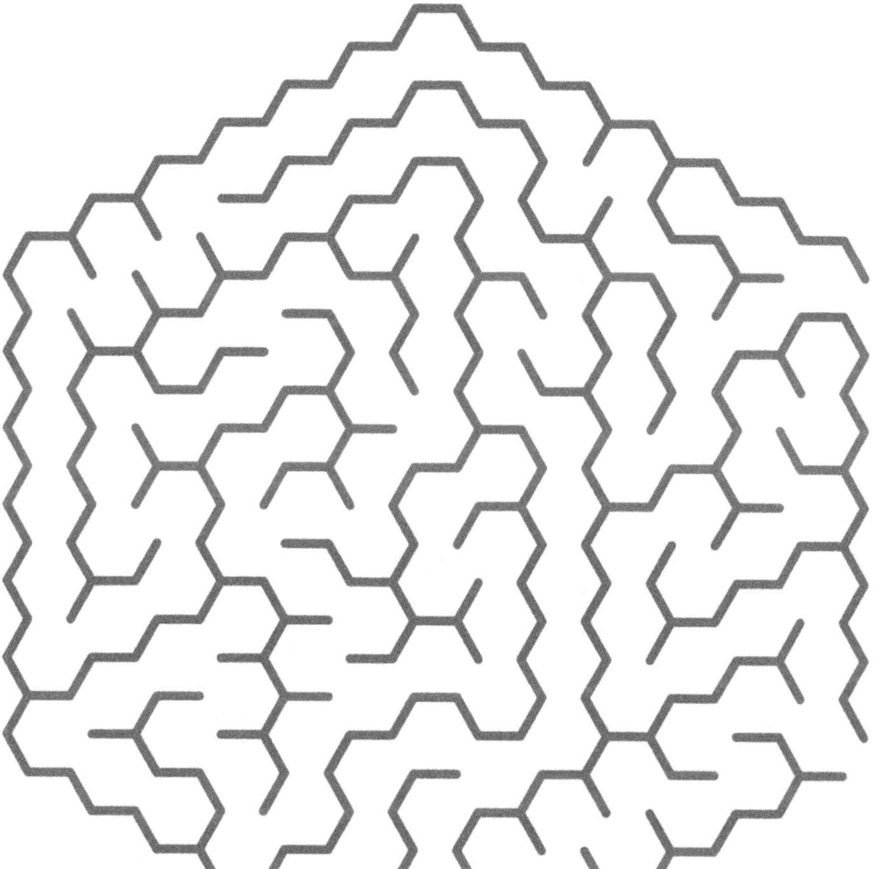

"You have within you right now, everything you need to deal with whatever the world can throw at you." - Brian Tracy

Sudoku

LEVEL: Easy

	7			1	9			
	5		6	4		7	3	
2		4	5	7	3			
		5			1		6	
	2		7	8	4	1		3
							2	9
3				5			8	
		6	1		2		7	
	4	2		3			9	6

Notes

Empowerment Odyssey

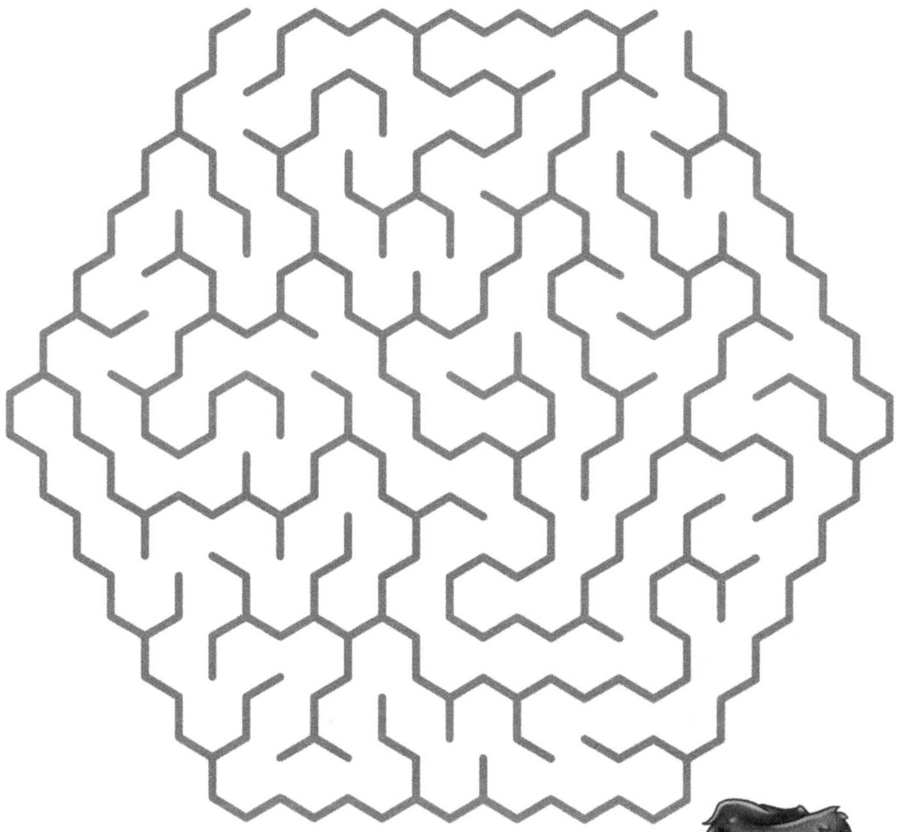

"The only way to do great work is to love what you do." - Steve Jobs

Self Criticism Worksheet

Critical Thought/s

What Triggered the Thought/s?

Any Physical and/or Emotional Sensations?

Letting Go Of

Self Criticism

Self Criticism Worksheet

Compassionate Thought

What would you say to a friend who expressed this thought?

A Year From Now

How will you feel about this event new year?

Concrete Plan

What actions can you take to prepare for this in the future?

Big Picture Plan

Imagine a future, free of this thought. What would you do?

NOTES

On The Go
Books
TK TCollection Publishing

Completed By:

Date:

ANSWERS

Across

[1] Opposite of stressed.

[2] A state of tranquility.

[3] Breathing and relaxation exercises.

[6] Feeling of appreciation.

[9] State of contentment and satisfaction .

Down

[4] Technique for reducing tension in muscles.

[5] Practise of being present.

[7] Technique involving controlled breathing patterns.

[8] process of mental reflection and introspection.

Across

[1] The ability to adapt well to stress and adversity.

[2] A mental state of being grateful or thankful.

[3] The practice of focusing one's mind and eliminating distractions.

[5] A relaxation technique involving controlled breathing.

Down

[6] The ability to manage one's emotions and reactions.

[7] A form of physical activity that boosts mental well-being.

[9] A state of inner peace and mental clarity.

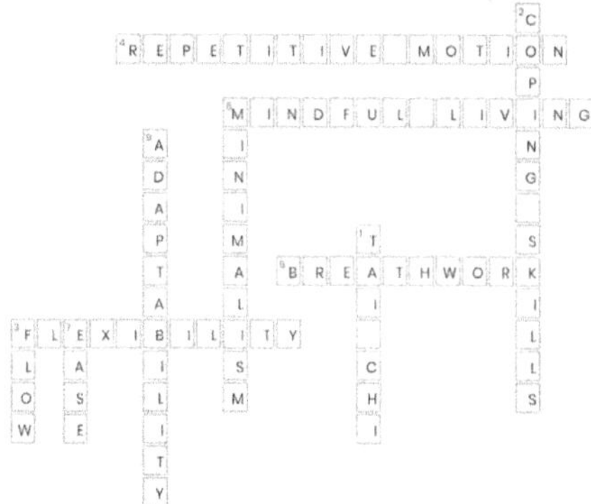

Across

[3] A technique for releasing tension through stretching.

[4] A method of clearing the mind through repetitive actions.

[5] A practice that involves controlled and intentional breathing.

[6] The act of slowing down and being present in the moment.

Down

[1] A technique to alleviate stress through rhythmic movements.

[2] The ability to cope with life's challenges.

[3] A state of being fully immersed and absorbed in an activity.

[6] An approach to reduce stress by simplifying life.

[7] A state of mental and physical relaxation.

[9] The ability to bounce back from difficult experiences.

Cryptograms

Hidden Figures

The Color Purple

Wonder Woman

Legally Blonde

Thelma and Louise

ANSWERS

Bee Amazing

Empowerment Journey

Trail of Confidence

Strength Maze Quest

Courageous Pathways

Empowered Passage

Maze of Fortitude

Inner Strength Route

Trailblazing Confidence

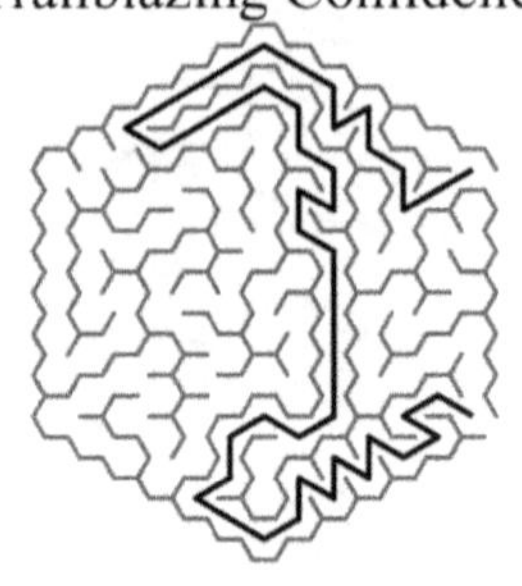

Empowerment Odyssey

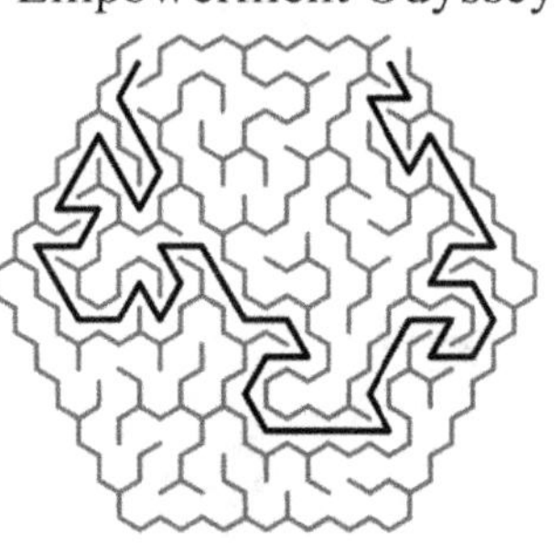

ANSWERS

9	7	8	6	3	1	2	4	5
2	3	5	4	9	8	6	1	7
6	4	1	7	2	5	8	9	3
7	1	9	5	8	6	4	3	2
3	8	6	2	1	4	7	5	9
4	5	2	9	7	3	1	8	6
1	9	7	3	4	2	5	6	8
5	2	4	8	6	9	3	7	1
8	6	3	1	5	7	9	2	4

3	6	2	9	1	7	4	8	5
7	5	9	4	3	8	1	6	2
8	4	1	6	2	5	9	7	3
1	8	7	3	5	4	2	9	6
4	9	6	2	8	1	3	5	7
5	2	3	7	6	9	8	1	4
6	3	8	5	9	2	7	4	1
2	1	4	8	7	6	5	3	9
9	7	5	1	4	3	6	2	8

9	1	3	5	4	6	2	8	7
8	7	6	1	2	3	5	4	9
4	5	2	9	7	8	6	1	3
7	9	1	2	6	4	8	3	5
2	3	4	8	5	7	9	6	1
6	8	5	3	9	1	4	7	2
5	4	8	7	3	2	1	9	6
3	6	9	4	1	5	7	2	8
1	2	7	6	8	9	3	5	4

5	1	4	6	2	7	9	3	8
6	9	7	3	5	8	4	1	2
3	8	2	1	4	9	6	7	5
2	7	5	9	3	6	1	8	4
1	3	8	4	7	2	5	9	6
9	4	6	5	8	1	3	2	7
7	6	3	2	9	4	8	5	1
8	5	1	7	6	3	2	4	9
4	2	9	8	1	5	7	6	3

7	8	9	6	2	5	4	1	3
6	5	3	9	4	1	2	8	7
1	2	4	7	8	3	5	9	6
2	1	7	4	5	9	3	6	8
9	4	6	8	3	7	1	2	5
8	3	5	2	1	6	7	4	9
3	7	8	1	6	4	9	5	2
4	9	2	5	7	8	6	3	1
5	6	1	3	9	2	8	7	4

6	9	3	7	1	2	8	4	5
7	1	4	5	3	8	2	9	6
5	8	2	6	9	4	1	7	3
9	4	5	3	6	1	7	2	8
3	2	6	8	4	7	5	1	9
8	7	1	9	2	5	6	3	4
2	5	7	4	8	3	9	6	1
4	6	8	1	7	9	3	5	2
1	3	9	2	5	6	4	8	7

7	8	1	5	9	4	6	3	2
4	9	3	7	6	2	1	5	8
5	6	2	3	1	8	9	4	7
3	1	9	6	4	7	8	2	5
6	2	7	8	5	1	4	9	3
8	5	4	9	2	3	7	1	6
1	3	5	4	8	6	2	7	9
9	4	8	2	7	5	3	6	1
2	7	6	1	3	9	5	8	4

8	7	3	2	1	9	6	4	5
9	5	1	6	4	8	7	3	2
2	6	4	5	7	3	9	1	8
4	3	5	9	2	1	8	6	7
6	2	9	7	8	4	1	5	3
7	1	8	3	6	5	4	2	9
3	9	7	4	5	6	2	8	1
5	8	6	1	9	2	3	7	4
1	4	2	8	3	7	5	9	6

TKTCollection
Publishing

Free Printable Downloads

Find lots of free printables in our freebies section.
Become a subscriber and receive them delivered to your inbox!

www.ingramcontent.com/pod-product-compliance
Lightning Source LLC
LaVergne TN
LVHW010939110826
845149LV00013B/2683

* 9 7 8 1 9 5 9 2 4 7 2 6 5 *